CRIME SCENE INVESTIGATION

CRACKING THE CODE WITH COMPUTERS

BY DONNA McKINNEY

BLASTOFF! DISCOVERY

LASTOFF! DISCOVERY, AN IMPRINT OF BELLWETHER MEDIA BY FLUTTERBEE

This edition first published in 2027 by Bellwether Media, Inc.

Bellwether Media is a division of FlutterBee Education Group.

For information regarding permission, write to Bellwether Media, Inc., Attention: Permissions Department,
3500 American Blvd W, Suite 150, Bloomington, MN 55431.

Library of Congress Cataloging-in-Publication Data is available at www.loc.gov or upon request from the publisher.

ISBN: 9798898800826 (hardcover)
ISBN: 9798898802066 (ebook)

Editor: Rachael Barnes Series Designer: Josh Brink

Printed in the United States of America, North Mankato, MN.

TABLE OF CONTENTS

WHAT IS DIGITAL FORENSICS?	4
DIGITAL EVIDENCE COLLECTION	12
SOLVING THE CRIME	18
THE FUTURE OF DIGITAL FORENSICS	26
GLOSSARY	30
TO LEARN MORE	31
INDEX	32

WHAT IS DIGITAL FORENSICS?

FORENSIC ANALYST

Computers and other digital devices are a daily part of life for many people. They support school, work, and play. But criminals can use these devices for **cybercrimes**. They often leave behind digital **evidence**.

Forensic analysts are like detectives. They solve cybercrimes. They collect digital evidence from computers and other devices. They analyze and preserve the evidence. Some evidence can be used in court cases. This work is known as digital forensics.

GOVERNMENT COMPUTER RECORD STORAGE IN THE 1970S

THAT IS A FIRST!

The first time a person was found guilty of a cybercrime was in 1981. The criminal hacked AT&T's company computers.

The earliest cybercrime happened before computers were invented. In 1834, two brothers tapped into the French **telegraph system**. They stole information to make money. Personal computers became popular in the early 1980s. This led to more cybercrimes. Digital forensics began around the same time.

The Federal Bureau of Investigation (FBI) started collecting digital evidence in 1984. Digital forensics gained more importance in the 1990s. Computer crimes rose in the 2000s. The digital forensics field grew too.

FBI PRESENTATION

STATS

CYBERCRIME TIPS REPORTED TO THE FBI

over **859,532** in **2024**

MONEY LOST IN CYBERCRIMES

$16.6 billion in **2024**

TOP WAYS FUNDS WERE LOST TO FRAUD IN 2024

cryptocurrency, wire transfers, debit cards and credit cards

GONE PHISHING

The cybercrime phishing sounds like the word fishing. Criminals "fish" for information that does not belong to them.

There are now many types of digital crimes. **Phishing** and **financial fraud** are the most common. Criminals also use computers for **hacking**. They can delete or change data on computers. They can create false information such as **deepfakes**.

Special areas of digital forensics work on different crimes. Some analysts study **network** activity. This includes internet use, messages, and emails. Others focus on mobile devices. They study cell phones and tablets. They also study smartwatches.

Many analysts study **database** activity. They may look at bank accounts to prove fraud. Forensic accounting tracks the flow of money to find fraud.

Forensic analysts help with state and federal cybercrime cases. Some local police have cybercrime teams. Others rely on state police or FBI teams.

POLICE OFFICER COLLECTING DIGITAL EVIDENCE

Several organizations in the United States focus on cybercrime. One group is made up of U.S. police and military teams. They protect the country from digital threats. Another group takes tips from the public about cybercrimes. Some government groups keep track of new technology. They share research with police around the world.

DIGITAL EVIDENCE COLLECTION

Analysts search devices to find evidence. Computers and cell phones are common devices. Analysts also search tablets and smartwatches. They find digital clues on **hard drives** and **servers**.

Data evidence reveals the activity on a computer system. Data shows when **suspects** were online. These clues show when a crime occurred. They might tell the methods used in the crime. Clues can reveal a suspect's location. They show a suspect's communications and web searches. Analysts follow these digital clues to solve crimes.

COMPUTER SERVERS

CELL PHONE EVIDENCE TAKEN APART FOR ANALYSIS

Forensic analysts often help police find digital evidence for other criminal cases. They review data from cell phones and social media. They preserve phone calls and text messages between suspects. They share images and videos from the time around the crime. They track suspects' location history.

Analysts review recordings from security cameras. They see if suspects were caught on camera entering or leaving crime scenes. Digital evidence can help police build a timeline of crimes and related suspects.

CASE FILE

MICHAEL JACKSON

CRIME death of Michael Jackson

YEAR OF THE CRIME 2009

HOW IT WAS SOLVED A doctor gave pop star Michael Jackson medicine that helps with sleep. Minutes later, Jackson died. His death shocked many. Police searched the doctor's computer. They found digital evidence. It proved that the doctor approved deadly amounts of the medicine for Jackson.

Analysts search for evidence in **software**. They also check online accounts and content. They are careful to preserve digital evidence. They take control of each device. They move each device off of networks onto hard drives. This prevents changes that might hide or delete evidence.

FORENSIC IMAGING HARDWARE

Next, they make forensic images. These are precise copies of data on each device. Forensic imaging **hardware** creates forensic images. The images have date stamps. This process keeps original data safe. Analysts use these images as they work.

SOLVING THE CRIME

REVIEWING EVIDENCE DATA

Next it is time to study the data. Analysts use software programs. The tools let them search data without changing it. Some programs look for hidden data. Other programs analyze data across several devices. Analysts also work on file carving. They use a program to find deleted files.

CRIME SCENE DO NOT CROSS

Some information cannot be seen when a device is shut down. Live analysis allows analysts to look at data while a suspect is using a device. This process also helps them find hidden data.

CASE FILE

CRIME Coreflood cyber fraud

YEARS OF THE CRIME 2001 to 2011

HOW IT WAS SOLVED In 2001, a harmful software called Coreflood was found on computers around the world. It let criminals steal personal information. This included passwords and banking information. The software spread to as many as two million computers. In 2011, the FBI tracked down the servers spreading the software. They shut down this long-running cybercrime!

Analysts must know **data privacy laws**. They complete their work while respecting personal privacy. Digital evidence may not be used in court if it is gathered incorrectly.

PRESENTING A DATA PRIVACY LAW

Analysts check the data. They compare forensic images to original data. They check that the images are accurate, exact copies of the originals. They might also change information into a text string called a hash. This makes it easy to make sure data is **authentic**.

Digital evidence can be used in court cases. Forensic analysts fill out forms to track the **chain of custody**. The forms list when the evidence was collected. They show how it has been stored. Chain of custody forms list the people who worked with the evidence. They show the evidence was not changed or deleted.

Then analysts prepare reports. They create charts and timelines. Analysts describe what they found. They explain methods used to collect data. These reports must be clear and accurate.

ENCASE FORENSIC

YEAR INVENTED

1998

WHAT IS IT?

EnCase Forensic is a forensic software tool. It helps analysts collect, preserve, and study digital evidence. It lets them work with a lot of data very quickly. It has helped solve many major cases. The evidence uncovered by EnCase is accurate enough to be used in court. It helps catch criminals.

Analysts' work must be fair and based on evidence. But two analysts can work with the same evidence and reach different conclusions. Police groups are working to improve this. They are creating standards for digital evidence training and review.

POLICE DIGITAL EVIDENCE COLLECTION TRAINING

CHALLENGES

AI TOOLS CAN HELP CRIMINALS

HUMAN ERROR

UNCLEAR CHAIN OF CUSTODY

Analysts are often called to court. They present their conclusions. They explain computer concepts. They use charts and images to show their work. Lawyers ask questions. They often ask how digital evidence was gathered. A suspect's lawyer may ask the judge to remove it if privacy laws were not followed. A judge or jury decides if the suspect is guilty.

THE FUTURE OF DIGITAL FORENSICS

The field of digital forensics is growing quickly. More devices connect to the internet than ever before. These include earbuds and doorbell cameras. Data from them can be used as evidence. **Artificial intelligence** (AI) is being used to quickly sort huge amounts of data. AI tools can find evidence across different devices.

Financial cybercrimes often have large amounts of bank data. AI tools can note unusual activity. Analysts also use AI to solve unsolved cases.

AI DEEPFAKE DETECTION SOFTWARE

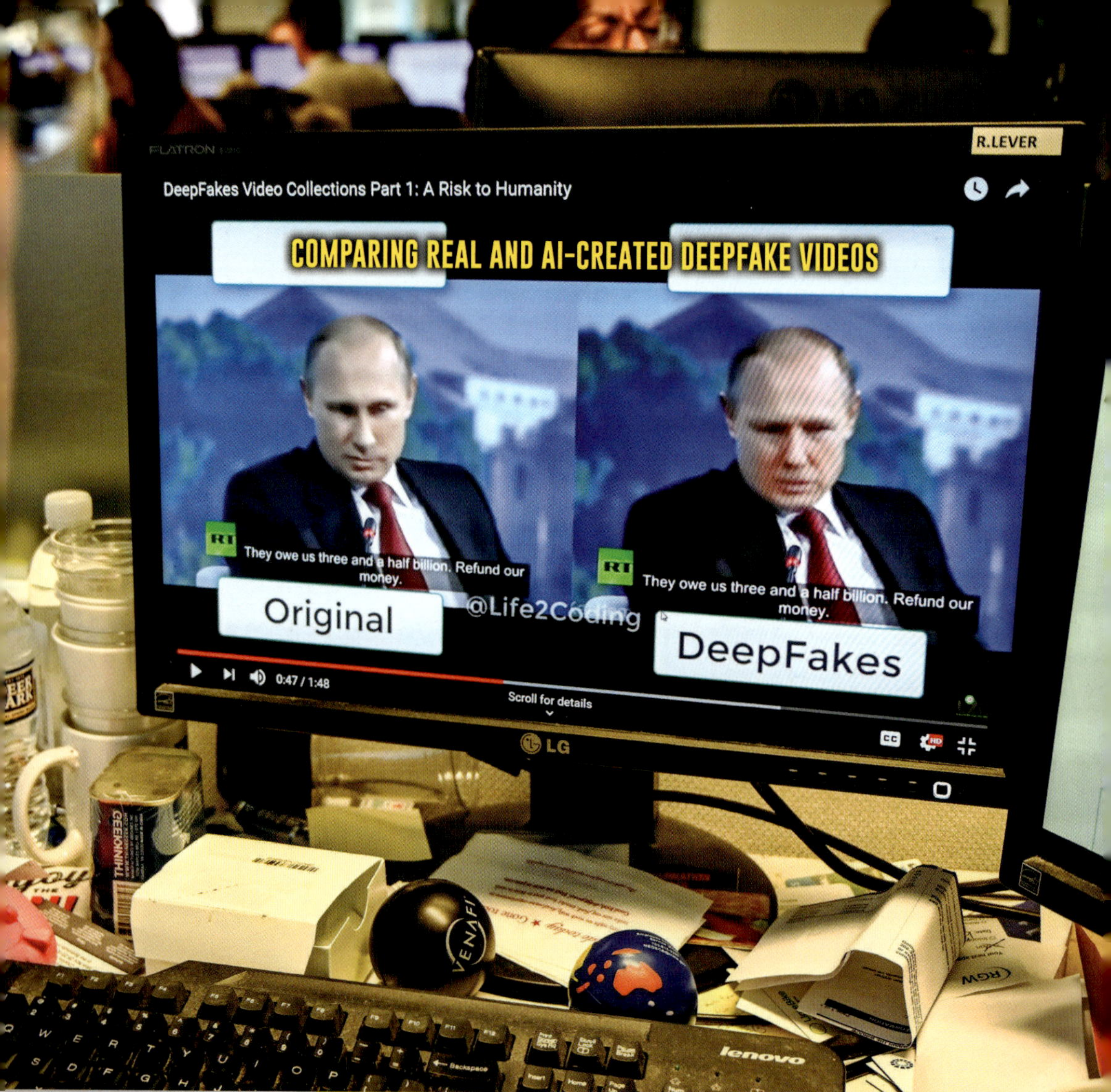

AI helps forensic analysts solve digital crimes. But AI also helps criminals. Criminals often use multiple devices for complex crimes. Analysts use AI crime-mapping tools to connect their digital activity. Criminals use AI to create deepfakes. Analysts can use AI to catch fakes! AI tools can help confirm which files are authentic.

Forensic analysts must use the latest forensic tools to catch criminals. AI finds important evidence. It filters out unimportant data. But it is up to analysts to put the pieces together to solve the crime. Case closed!

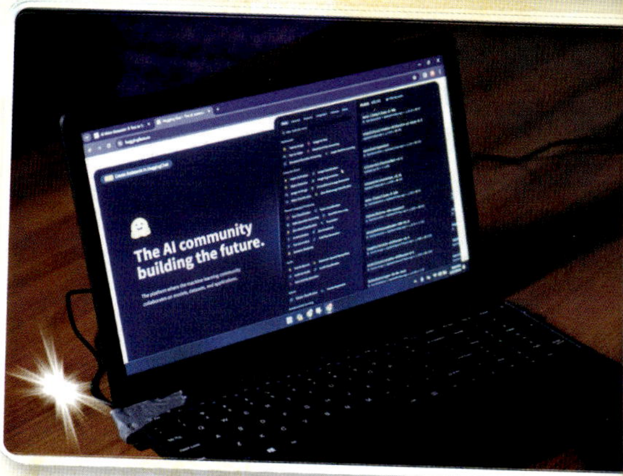

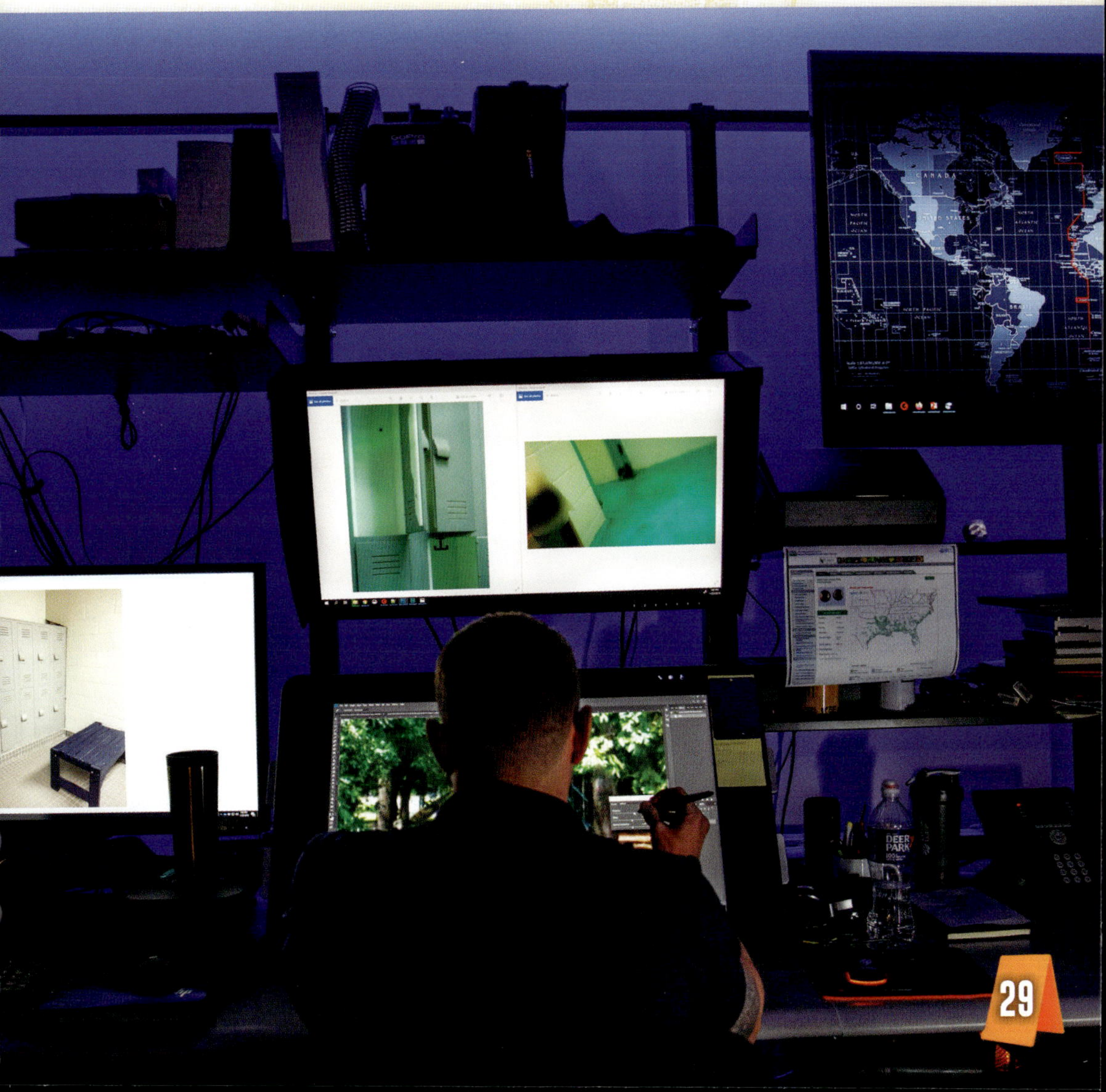

GLOSSARY

artificial intelligence–a computer's ability to do things a human mind can do

authentic–real, not fake or copied

chain of custody–the written record of everyone who handles a piece of evidence from the time it is collected until it goes to court

cybercrimes–crimes committed using computers and the internet

data privacy laws–rules that protect a person's ability to control their personal data and who has access to it

database–related to a digital system used to store and sort data

deepfakes–images, audio, or video that are manipulated using AI

evidence–a witness statement, an item or impression found at a crime scene, or digital data that links a suspect to a crime

financial fraud–purposefully tricking a person or company in order to steal money

forensic analysts–people who use scientific methods to study digital evidence

hacking–the act of gaining or trying to gain illegal access to a computer or computer system

hard drives–parts inside computers that store data

hardware–parts of a computer that people can touch

network–related to hardware that connects devices

phishing–the practice of tricking people into sharing personal information on the internet

servers–computers in networks that provide services to other computers in the network

software–computer programs that do specific tasks

suspects–people the police believe may have committed a crime

telegraph system–a system that sent messages at a distance through coded signals

CROSS CRIME SCENE DO NOT CRO

TO LEARN MORE

AT THE LIBRARY

Hamilton, John. *Forensics.* Minneapolis, Minn.: Abdo Publishing, 2022.

Hatalla, Meghan. *12 Incredible Facts About Cybercriminals.* Mankato, Minn.: Black Rabbit Books, 2026.

Haynes, Danielle. *What Does the FBI Do?* Buffalo, N.Y.: PowerKids Press, 2026.

ON THE WEB

FACTSURFER

Factsurfer.com gives you a safe, fun way to find more information.

1. Go to www.factsurfer.com.
2. Enter "cracking the code with computers" into the search box and click 🔍.
3. Select your book cover to see a list of related content.

INDEX

artificial intelligence (AI), 27, 28, 29
case file, 15, 19
chain of custody, 22
challenges, 24, 25, 28
court, 5, 20, 22, 25
data privacy laws, 20, 25
deepfakes, 8, 27, 28
digital forensics, 5, 6, 7, 9, 27
EnCase Forensic, 23
evidence, 5, 7, 10, 12, 13, 14, 15, 16, 18, 20, 22, 24, 25, 27, 29
Federal Bureau of Investigation (FBI), 7, 10, 11
forensic analysts, 4, 5, 9, 10, 12, 13, 14, 15, 16, 17, 18, 19, 20, 21, 22, 23, 24, 25, 27, 28, 29
forensic images, 17, 21
hard drives, 12, 16
history, 6, 7
servers, 12, 13
stats, 7
suspects, 13, 14, 15, 19, 25
tools, 17, 18, 19, 23, 27, 28, 29

The images in this book are reproduced through the courtesy of: FBI media/ Federal Bureau of Investigation, front cover, pp. 5, 6, 7, 9 (top), 10, 11, 13, 16-17, 17, 20 (top), 21 (top); Jeff McCollough, pp. 2 (evidence marker 1), 3 (evidence marker 3); Uri, p. 3 (evidence marker 2); Hyoung Chang/ The Denver Post/ Getty Images, pp. 4-5; Andrey_Popov, p. 7 (stats top); ESB Professional, p. 7 (stats middle); EugeneEdge, p. 7 (stats bottom); PR Image Factory, p. 8; Nicolas Armer/ picture alliance/ Getty Images, pp. 9, 14; Lori Van Buren/ Albany Times Union/ Getty Images, p. 10 (top); Philipp Schulze/ picture alliance/ Getty Images, p. 12 (top); Microgen, p. 12; khamkula, p. 13 (top); Roslan RAHMAN/ AFP/ Getty Images, pp. 14 (top), 26-27; Pressmaster, p. 15 (top); Larry Davis, Los Angeles Times/ Wikimedia Commons, p. 15; Lynn DeBruin/ AP Images, p. 18; dpa picture alliance/ Alamy Stock Photo, p. 19 (top); Summit Art Creations, p. 19; Don Thompson/ AP Images, p. 20; Prathankarnpap, p. 21; Spencer Weiner/ Los Angeles Times/ Getty Images, p. 22; Rachel Leathe/ AP Images, p. 23 (top); Fairfax Media/ Getty Images, p. 23; Anne Cusack/ Los Angeles Times/ Getty Images, p. 24 (top); Kim Kulish/ Corbis/ Getty Images, p. 24; BOY ANTHONY, p. 25 (top left); DC Studio, p. 25 (top right); AnnaStills, p. 25 (bottom); Joshua Boucher/ The State/ Pool/ Tribune News Service/ Getty Images, p. 25; Chris Jung/ AP Images, p. 27; ALEXANDRA ROBINSON/ AFP/ Getty Images, p. 28; Matthew Hinton/ AP Images, p. 29 (top); Jacquelyn Martin/ AP Images, p. 29.